CHAMPION SPORT

BIOGRAPHIES

JACQUES VILLENEUVE

CHAMPION SPORT

BIOGRAPHIES

JACQUES VILLENEUVE

KEN SPARLING

W

Warwick Publishing Inc.
Toronto   Los Angeles
www.warwickgp.com

We acknowledge the financial support of the Government of Canada through the Book Publishing Industry Development Program for our publishing activities.

ISBN: 1-894020-57-X

Published by Warwick Publishing Inc.
162 John Street, Suite 300, Toronto, Ontario, Canada M5V 2E5

Cover and layout design: Heidi Gemmill
Editorial Services: Joseph Romain

Printed and bound in Canada

Cover and interior photos courtesy AP/Wide World Photos

Table of Contents

A Note about Pronunciation

The final "s" in French names such as "Gilles" and "Jacques" is usually silent. The name "Gilles" is pronounced something like "szheel" and "Jacques" is pronounced "szhock."

Factsheet

Jacques Villeneuve

Birth Date: April 9, 1971

Birthplace: St.-Jean-sur-Richelieu, Quebec, Canada

Residence: Monaco/Switzerland

Career Highlights:

1988　first formal auto race, Italian Touring Car Championship

1991　6th in Italian Formula 3 Championship series

1992　2nd in Japanese F3 Championship series

1993　3rd in Toyota Atlantic championship; named rookie of the year.

1994　2nd in Indianapolis 500; named IndyCar rookie of the year

1995　youngest ever IndyCar champion

1996　2nd in F1 World Championship

1997　wins F1 World Championship

Jacques Villeneuve Firsts:

- first Canadian Indy 500 winner
- first driver ever to win four races in his first F1 season
- first Canadian Formula One World Champion, 1997
- first driver ever to win all three of the most prestigious titles in the racing world: the Indy 500, the IndyCar Championship and the Formula One World Championship

Introduction

1

On the weekend of the first Formula One Grand Prix automobile race of the 1997 season, a 5-foot 6-inch (168-cm), rather mousy-looking 24-year-old arrived in the city square of Melbourne, Australia. This grungy, bespectacled young man wearing jeans and a lumberjack shirt had come, along with a police escort, to greet his fans.

The mob scene that followed might have made you think Mel Gibson was home for a visit, or that a rock star was making a personal appearance before a big concert. Many of the fans in the crowd were teenage girls come to worship their idol. But this idol was no rock star. This was Formula One race car driver Jacques Villeneuve.

Some journalists are a bit mystified by Villeneuve's popularity. He's not your typical Formula One driver. Most newspaper and magazine articles about Formula One talk about how the drivers are performing on the race track—who passed who, who crashed into what. With Villeneuve, journalists often find themselves discussing the color of his hair (which has changed a number of times since he joined Formula One) or his latest opinion about the Formula One establishment.

Villeneuve is like a breath of fresh air. In the world of Formula One, where many of the key players take their business pretty seriously, Jacques is a lot fun. He shows up at interviews and other events dressed in "high grunge" outfits. He says what he thinks. On top of all this, he just happens to be a great race car driver.

Villeneuve gets about a hundred letters a day, most of them from females between the ages of 13 and 24. He has a number of Internet Web sites devoted to him. He has fan clubs all over the world. There are several books about Jacques, including one he wrote himself.

In some ways, Villeneuve's success is not so surprising. Formula One (F1) is considered by many to be the pinnacle of automobile racing. Making it to F1 is the greatest possible form of success for a race car driver. But Jacques Villeneuve's great ability as a race car driver was evident long before he made it to Formula One. He had a stunningly successful, if short, career racing IndyCars in 1994 and 1995. Before that, he did quite well in a series known as Formula Atlantic.

Some would argue that Jacques's success has a lot to do with the Villeneuve name. He comes from a family of racers, the most famous being his father, the late

Gilles Villeneuve. Gilles raced a Formula One car for the legendary Ferrari team up until his death in a crash in 1982. Although he never managed to take the Formula One world championship, Gilles inspired great devotion from his fans through his fearless (some would say reckless) driving style.

Having the Villeneuve name has been both a blessing and a curse for Jacques. Being a Villeneuve has given Jacques opportunities that most race car drivers can only dream of. But it has also put Jacques under a great deal of pressure to prove himself.

Becoming a successful race car driver does not happen overnight, and Jacques's first attempts at racing were far from successful. As with any difficult endeavor, it takes time and effort to become a good racer. It also takes a measure of talent, and having the Villeneuve name was never a guarantee that Jacques had talent.

Gilles Villeneuve's high profile in the racing world means that comparisons between father and son are inevitable. But just as Jacques has his own way of dressing and behaving, he also has his own style of racing. In some ways his style has made him a much more successful and enduring race car driver than his father was.

Jacques himself will tell you that he has no desire to out-perform his father. He is always happy to hear stories about what a great driver his father was, and he is proud to bear the Villeneuve name. But he insists he is his own man and he dislikes being compared constantly to his father Gilles.

Perhaps it is the unavoidable comparisons that have driven Jacques to stay away from the media sometimes. While other drivers are generally quite eager to discuss their careers with sports reporters, Jacques is much less inclined to talk. His desire to keep to himself has made him something of a mystery.

There's a Formula One video game based on the 1997 race season. It allows players to choose from the actual race tracks, the actual Formula One teams, and all the actual drivers—all the drivers, that is, except one. When a player chooses to drive for the Williams-Renault team (the team Villeneuve drove for in 1997) the driver who appears on the TV screen has no face and no name.

In some ways, Villeneuve is like this nameless, faceless video game character. The details of his life— his birthday, the schools he went to, the types of cars he's raced—are there for all to see. But the man behind the details is a little harder to discover.

Chapter 1

Born To Race

When Jacques Villeneuve moved to Japan in the early 1990s, he was reported to have gone out one day and spent thousands of dollars in just a few hours to get a sound system and computer equipment for his new apartment.

Jacques's family has been wealthy since Jacques was a teenager. He went to an exclusive boarding school in the mountains of Switzerland. He has lived much of his life in Monaco, home to many of the world's rich and famous.

But life for Jacques Villeneuve was not always so glamorous. Born on Good Friday, April 9, 1971, Jacques began his life in a small town called Saint-Jean-Sur-Richelieu in the Canadian province of Quebec. The year Jacques was born, his father, Gilles Villeneuve, won the Quebec snowmobile racing championship; a year later he won it again.

Winning snowmobile races in little towns in Quebec is hardly a way to get rich, and Gilles

Villeneuve had no other means of earning money. Jacques's early years were spent living in a mobile home on a piece of land across the road from Gilles's parents' rural house.

The Villeneuves used an overturned oil drum for a front doorstep. While Gilles was away for days, sometimes weeks at a time, racing snowmobiles across the province of Quebec and beyond, his wife Joann was under their home with a blow torch trying to unfreeze the water pipes.

In the spring of 1973, Gilles decided to apply his talent for controlling vehicles at high speeds to the automobile racing circuit. The switch to racing cars was an important decision in the life of the Villeneuves. It determined not only how Gilles's life would turn out, but how his son Jacques's life would turn out as well.

The same year Gilles began racing cars, on July 26, 1973, Jacques's sister Melanie was born. Having two young children made life even more difficult for Joann Villeneuve, who had no means of transportation while her husband was away at races. If she needed to get into town to shop or for an appointment, she had to take a taxi and she had to bring the children along. During the cold, snowy Quebec winters, Joann often had to dig herself out of the mobile home before she could go anywhere.

In 1974, despite vigorous protests from his wife,

Gilles sold the mobile home to buy a racing car. At this point, Jacques Villeneuve's life began to resemble that of a gypsy child. With no home of their own, the Villeneuves traveled around the country in a camper towed by a pickup truck that Gilles had borrowed from his father. When they weren't traveling with Gilles, Jacques and his mother and sister stayed with relatives.

By 1976, Gilles was racing in a series called Formula Atlantic. Formula Atlantic cars are single-seat, open-cockpit racers similar to, but much less powerful than the cars used in the highest level of racing in the world, Formula One. Gilles wanted, eventually, to become a Formula One driver, so Formula Atlantic was an obvious step in the right direction.

By this point in his career, Gilles had purchased a motorhome and his family traveled together everywhere across North America to race meets. The Villeneuve motorhome became a familiar sight in the paddock, the area near the track where the drivers stay during a race weekend.

Jacques couldn't help but learn a lot about the racing business from an early age. While his father was out spinning the wheels on his Formula Atlantic car, Jacques was in the paddock spinning the wheel on his tricycle, or playing with the toy cars his father often bought for him.

Gilles was immensely successful in the Formula

Atlantic series. By the end of 1977 he had been signed to drive for the most famous Formula One race team in the world, Ferrari. This was great news for Gilles, but it meant he would have to move his family to Europe.

One of the main reasons Formula One racing is such a high-profile sport is that, over the course of a race season, the drivers race at tracks all over the world—North America, South America, Asia, Australia, Britain and continental Europe. The Canadian Grand Prix takes place in Montreal, not far from where Gilles and Jacques were both born. There were also a few races in the United States in the 1970s.

But the majority of Formula One races run in and around Europe. The team Gilles was driving for, Ferrari, was located in Italy. So the Villeneuves decided to make Europe their new home.

Rather than move to Ferrari's home country, however, Gilles decided to settle in France, which is right next door to Italy. It was a long drive to work, several hours in fact, but France had a great advantage over Italy in Gilles's eyes. Living in France would be easier for the French-speaking Villeneuves. Gilles was also intent on seeing Jacques and Melanie educated in the French language.

Europeans take their automobile racing very seriously, and many European race fans, particularly the Italians, are great supporters of Ferrari. As Ferrari's newest driver, Gilles became a celebrity almost overnight.

Members of the European press were eager to come up with as much information as they could about the new member of the Ferrari team. In interviews, Gilles often talked about his family.

"Jacques is six and already he knows how to hold a steering wheel," he once told reporters. "He sits on my knees, I press the accelerator and he drives. We are already up to 60 miles an hour."

A few years later, the Villeneuves moved to the glamorous Principality of Monaco, a tiny country on the southeast coast of France, near the Italian border. Monaco is known for its royal family, its casinos, its sunny climate, its liberal tax laws, and its Formula One Grand Prix race. For the Villeneuves it offered the advantages of being closer to Ferrari's home base in Italy, and having French as its official language.

By the time Jacques was 11 years old, he had stopped watching his father race, because it made him too nervous. At the 1981 Monaco Grand Prix, Gilles's final race through the streets where he lived, Jacques had to leave because he developed a terrible headache, reportedly because he was so nervous.

All the changes in Jacques's life—the moving around, the new-found riches and a proper family home—were nothing compared to the change Jacques was going to experience in 1982. Five races into the

Formula One season, while attempting to qualify for the Belgian Grand Prix at a circuit called Zolder, Gilles Villeneuve hit the back of another car. His car was sent cartwheeling into the fence. Gilles did not survive the crash.

Chapter 2

Prince of the Road

To say that Jacques Villeneuve was born to race is like saying a prince is born to be a king. Being born the son of a king means that you will probably one day become a king yourself, but it does not necessarily mean you'll be a good king. Having Gilles Villeneuve for a father was certainly no guarantee that Jacques Villeneuve would turn out to be a great race car driver.

When Jacques was a little boy and someone asked him what he wanted to be when he grew up, he would say he wanted to race cars just like his dad. His father used to give him toy cars to play with and, according to his mother, these were the only toys that really interested him.

Jacques claims that he doesn't have any really strong memories of his father racing cars. He has said that he remembers other things, like Christmas, and telling his father to go faster and faster when they were out together in a car or a truck or their boat.

Certainly, Jacques himself showed no interest in

racing while his father was still alive. Unlike some race car drivers who begin their careers driving go-karts when they are still in primary school, Jacques did no formal racing until he was in his teens.

But Gilles left behind a legacy that would propel Jacques into racing almost in spite of himself. Gilles also left behind a great deal of money.

When he first started racing for Ferrari, Gilles made about $75,000 a year. By the time of his final full season of racing in 1981, Ferrari was paying him $300,000 annually.

Gilles was also making a great deal of money from sponsors. In his original deal with Ferrari, he had managed to set things up so he owned his driving suit. This meant that any advertiser wanting to put their logo on Gilles's suit paid Gilles directly. Ferrari got none of that money. Gilles wore ads for Labatt beer, Giacobazzi wine, Marlboro cigarettes, Champion sparkplugs, Michelin tires, Smeg kitchen appliances, and other merchandise.

Why would the Marlboro cigarette company, or any company for that matter, want to pay $100,000 to have their logo on Gilles Villeneuve's driving suit? For every Formula One race, hundreds of journalists generate tens of thousands of articles and photographs for newspapers and magazines around the globe. About a half billion people in over a hundred countries watch Formula One races on TV. At the height of his career, in the early 1980s, Gilles was one of the highest profile Formula One drivers on the circuit. There were potentially a great many people who might notice the Marlboro name on Gilles's driving suit.

In addition to his salary and the money he earned from sponsors, Gilles got money for each point he earned in a race. When he won the Canadian Grand Prix in 1978, for example, he earned an $81,000 bonus, $9,000 for each of the 9 points a driver earned in 1978 for winning a race.

Despite the fact that he spent a lot of his money on "toys" like a boat, a helicopter, an expensive camera and a pool for his home, Gilles left his wife, Joann, with a great deal of money. After her husband died, Joann was able to send Jacques to an exclusive private boarding school called Beausoleil, which is located high up in the Alps mountain range in Switzerland. Jacques attended Beausoleil from the time he was 12 to the time he was 17.

Considering he had recently lost his father, it is not surprising that Jacques was a bit difficult to handle during his time at Beausoleil. According to his teachers, he was very bright, but also very headstrong and independent.

Yula de Meyer, who ran the school at the time Jacques attended, told Villeneuve biographer Timothy Collings that, although Jacques usually did as he was told, he questioned everything. "If he did not want to study," says de Meyer, "because it was not interesting to him, then he would not study."

Beausoleil was where Jacques met Craig Pollock, who later went on to manage Jacques's racing career. Pollock was a teacher at Beausoleil at the time. He has described Jacques as an energetic and determined student who had the "killer instinct." According to Pollock, Jacques never got involved in a competition just for the fun of it—he always wanted to win.

At the time Jacques entered Beausoleil, there was still no strong indication that he wanted to be a race car driver. There are those who will claim that Jacques probably knew all along what he wanted to do, he just didn't talk about. This fits Jacques's personality, which comes across as very calculating at times, but in a quiet and often introverted way.

Jacques himself will tell you he was not born to race. "Racing is not like a gene that you can inherit," he has said. "But when you come from a family where racing was always there, you get used to speed at an early age."

In September 1985, when he was 14, Jacques was given the opportunity to race go-karts at a track in Italy called the Autodromo Enzo e Dino Ferrari. There is little doubt that this opportunity came about because of his name. Italians are great racing fans, and Gilles Villeneuve is their number one favorite Formula One driver of all time.

When Jacques was 15, he attended a three-day course at the Jim Russell driving school, the same school his father had attended. Whether or not Jacques had inherited his father's ability as a race car driver was yet to be seen, but the one thing that Jacques did inherit from his father was his small stature. Staff at the driving school had to put blocks on the pedals of one of the Formula Fords they used so Jacques's feet could reach them.

Accounts of Jacques's first stint driving a race car are somewhat inconclusive. He did well enough to pass the driving course, but there was no reason to believe he was going to become a world champion.

Jacques spent the summer of his sixteenth year at the Spenard-David Racing School in Shannonville, Ontario, Canada. He didn't have the kind of money it would take to attend the school and he wasn't getting any financial support from his mother. Joann wanted Jacques to finish his schooling at Beausoleil before he launched into a racing career. While she certainly did not forbid him to attend the racing school, she refused to pay for the course.

However, Jacques was determined. The racing school had a mechanics' training program that allowed a student to learn to race in return for doing some work in the garage. School owner David Spenard says that in the end, "Jacques didn't do much work." It turned out he had no real interest in working on cars—as Spenard put it, he "didn't like to get his hands dirty"—so, while the other students worked on the cars to pay their keep, Jacques was put to work painting the garage.

Jacques's first formal racing was in the Italian Touring Car Championship of 1988 where he competed in three races. He drove a car called an Alfa Romeo 33 which was not much more than a road car. He did three races, but he claims the car was terrible and he prefers to forget the experience altogether.

Whether it was the car, or Jacques's lack of experience, he did not do very well in his first formal racing series. He finished 10th in his first race, 14th in the final race, and not at all in the other.

Racing on weekends left Jacques little time to keep up with his studies and, at the age of 17, Jacques was asked by the staff at Beausoleil to leave the school. His mother was not happy to see her son follow in his father's footsteps, but at the same time she knew she could not stop him from doing what he seemed so determined to do.

"If he wants to be world champion," Joann said at the time, "he will fight like heck and he will probably do it."

After leaving Beausoleil, Jacques entered the Italian Formula Three Championship series. It took him a while to catch on, but at the end of the 1991 F3 season, he was the sixth-best driver in the series.

Jacques himself admits that he was far from professional when he started out his racing career. "I was a young kid having fun," Villeneuve told *Saturday Night* magazine. "The older drivers on the circuit were a bit tougher on themselves...I was just a kid playing, basically."

In 1991, while attending the Monaco Grand Prix in Monte Carlo as a spectator, Jacques ran into Craig Pollock, his former teacher from the Beausoleil school. Jacques discovered that Pollock had given up teaching and was working in the motor sports industry.

Not long after their meeting in Monte Carlo, Jacques turned up in Switzerland to ask Pollock to be his manager. Pollock resisted. But Jacques showed up again, and then again. The third time he showed up he told Pollock, "I like you, you're my friend...You should become my manager because I'm lucky, and if you become my manager that will probably rub off on you." Pollock gave in and agreed to manage Jacques's career.

In 1992, Pollock entered Jacques in the Japanese Formula Three series where Jacques chalked up three wins and finished second in the championship. Pollock claims that the Japanese series is the most competitive F3 series going and that Jacques learned a lot from this experience.

By now Jacques was beginning to draw some attention in racing circles. Like his father, he was a fast and capable race car driver. But Jacques was cool, almost calculating, and his manner on the track was very consistent, whereas his father's recklessness had made him much less reliable.

"Gilles drove with fire and emotion and great skill," wrote Len Coates in the *Globe and Mail*. Coates went on to describe Jacques as driving with "a calculated coolness and his emotions in check. It's the difference between driving with your heart and driving with your head."

In 1993, Jacques was hired by a man named Barry Green who was at that time part owner of the Forsythe-Green Ralt Racing Team. This was to be Jacques's big break in the racing world. Green entered Jacques in a series called the Toyota Atlantic Championship, and Jacques did quite well. He was third in the championship after winning five races and he was named rookie of the year.

But the real break came the following year when Forsythe-Green decided to enter the IndyCar racing series.

Chapter 3

Prince of Power

Jacques's IndyCar boss, Barry Green, once called Jacques "the smoothest driver...I've ever worked with." Green was amazed at the quality of the feedback Jacques was able to give his team of mechanics, especially considering Jacques had been driving for only five years.

Before signing Villeneuve to race for his team, Barry Green had worked with a number of very successful race car drivers, many of them the sons of race car drivers. He worked with 1991 IndyCar champion Michael Andretti, whose father Mario had won the 1978 Formula One world championship as well as IndyCar championships in 1965, 1966, 1969 and 1984. Green had also worked with Al Unser, Jr., who won the 1990 and 1994 IndyCar series and whose father, Al senior, had won it in 1970, 1983 and 1985. Al junior's uncle, Bobby Unser, was IndyCar champion in 1968 and 1974.

"They've all been brought up around racing," Green says of the younger Andretti, Unser and Villeneuve. "I guess you get horribly used to it."

Green made the move from the Atlantic Formula series to IndyCars by securing the sponsorship of a large tobacco company called Players Ltd. Getting a high-profile sponsor was a major coup, particularly when you consider that the cost of fielding an IndyCar for a single season was about $13 million.

During his rookie year racing in the IndyCar series, Jacques's car carried the number 27, the same number as his father's Formula One Ferrari had carried. Perhaps this was good luck, because Jacques's first year racing IndyCars was hugely successful. He was named rookie of the year and he placed second in the Indianapolis 500, arguably the most famous race in all of motorsports.

At the end of the season, Jacques was sixth in the points standings, but more important, he had won a race. In the third-last race of the season, at the Road America circuit in Wisconsin, he held off veteran drivers Al Unser and Emerson Fittipaldi to cross the finish line first.

Jacques said winning at Road America was a real pleasure because it is such an enjoyable track to drive. Unlike the ovals included in the IndyCar series, where the drivers basically go around and around in a circle for hundreds of miles, Road America is a road circuit, a combination of high-speed straights and curves, as well as some low-speed corners where a driver is forced to break heavily.

After Jacques won his first IndyCar race, two-time Formula One world champion Fittipaldi said, "He did a fantastic job. The last 10 laps with pressure from Al and me, he never made a mistake. He showed a lot of maturity." Fittipaldi went on to compare Jacques to his late father, claiming, as others had before him, that Jacques was a more consistent driver than Gilles.

At the end of the 1994 season, other IndyCar teams were showing an interest in Villeneuve, as were some Formula One teams. Villeneuve, however, decided to stay in IndyCars for another season, because he thought it was a better series with more opportunities.

By the time the 1995 IndyCar series began in Miami, Barry Green had taken over the team completely and renamed it Team Green. As the cars lined up to start the first race of the season, Jacques and Team Green were a little concerned, because the car had not performed well during winter testing.

They needn't have worried. Jacques worked his way up from eighth at the start of the race to third place by about halfway through. Two-thirds of the way through the race, Jacques pulled in for a pit stop and Team Green did a fantastic job of getting him back out onto the track quickly. He took the lead and kept it, fighting off some fierce competitors to win the first race of the season.

Villeneuve scored points in two of the next four races, but failed to finish the other two. Race five was the Indianapolis 500 (the "Indy"), the most popular motor race in the United States.

In most types of automobile racing, including IndyCars, drivers must participate in an event known as "qualifying" before they can actually compete in a race. Besides eliminating teams that are not fast enough to compete, the main reason for qualifying is to determine the positions the drivers will take on the track at the start of the race. Automobile race tracks are much too narrow for all the cars to start the race side by side, the way runners start out in a foot race.

During qualifying, each car comes out onto the track to do some laps, and these laps are timed. The driver tries to go around the track as fast as possible. When qualifying is through, the fastest driver gets to be first in line when the actual race begins. The second fastest driver starts next to him. The third and fourth fastest drivers start side by side behind the fastest two, and so on to the back of the line.

The Indy 500 is a little different in that the cars line up in rows of three, but otherwise, qualifying for Indianapolis is the same as it is at any other IndyCar race.

Jacques qualified fifth for the 79th annual

Indianapolis 500. This put him in the center of the second row for the start of the 500-mile (804-km) race that covers 200 laps of the Indianapolis Motor Speedway. Today, the Indy 500 is no longer part of the series of races Jacques participated in during the 1994 and 1995 racing seasons, but back then it was considered the jewel of the IndyCar series.

On lap 37 of the 1995 race, a yellow flag came out because there was some debris on the track. This meant the drivers had to slow down and follow the pace car and no one was allowed to pass. Unfortunately, Jacques got a little too eager and passed the pace car just before it pulled off the track so that racing could resume.

Jacques was penalized two laps, a terrible blow which meant that in order to finish the race, Jacques would have to drive his car five miles (eight kilometres) farther than any of the other drivers. But it was still early in the race and Team Green had not given up. Over the course of the next 30 laps, Jacques tore around the track fast enough to make up one of the lost laps. It took him nearly another 60 circuits to make up the other, but by lap 156 he had taken the lead.

By the time the yellow flag came out again on lap 185, another Canadian driver, Scott Goodyear, had taken the lead away from Jacques. Goodyear's car was faster than Villeneuve's, and it looked like the race was his. But then, as the pace car pulled off this time,

Goodyear was the one who passed it before it was off the track. He was black-flagged, meaning he had to pull into the pit lane and stay there for a 10-second penalty to elapse before re-joining the race.

Villeneuve led the last 10 laps of the race and crossed the finish line first. He had won the Indianapolis 500 in just his second season racing IndyCars.

Jacques went on to have a great season, winning two more races and scoring points in all but one of the others. It was obvious to everyone in the racing world that Villeneuve had arrived.

Jacques could have easily carried on successfully for a number of years in IndyCars. But it was clear that while he enjoyed racing IndyCars, he saw them as inferior to Formula One. He wanted to prove himself in what many consider to be the greatest form of motor racing in the world.

In August 1995, during a break in the IndyCar series, Villeneuve flew to England to test drive a Formula One car for a team called Williams-Renault, one of the top European racing teams. Villeneuve called the tests "very conclusive" and he immediately signed a contract to drive for Williams in 1996.

Barry Green would be sorry to see Jacques go, but he understood that such a great driver needed to seek new challenges. Upon hearing that Jacques was moving to Formula One, Green said that his team was proud to have made such "a significant contribution" to the development of Jacques's career.

Despite the fact that he would be leaving Team Green at the end of the year, Jacques was determined to do the best job he could for the remainder of the season. He finished the 1995 IndyCar series in style, chalking up more points than any other driver that year, thereby becoming the IndyCar series champion.

Jacques said that winning the series meant a lot to him. "This is my first championship in any series," he told reporters, "so it is special."

In 1996, Jacques would prove that he was a top-class driver not only in North America, but all over the world, as he joined the international racing world of Formula One.

Chapter 4

The Difference Between IndyCar and F1

In 1957 and 1958, the Race of Two Worlds was held at a race track in Italy called Monza. The race pitted IndyCars against Formula One cars in an effort to see which performed better. Both times, the IndyCars won.

The two types of cars have not competed against each other since, and the debate about which type of racing is better rages on. IndyCar fans say that Indy racing is faster and more competitive, with more cars passing each other throughout the course of a race. Formula One fans, on the other hand, will tell you that F1 cars are more sophisticated and that Formula One Grand Prix racing is a more subtle form of competition that involves more strategy and greater technological advances.

IndyCars definitely have a higher top speed. On long oval tracks, like the Indianapolis Motor Speedway, the cars reach speeds well in excess of 200 mph (321 km/h). But on twisting, turning road race tracks, Formula One cars perform better because they corner faster.

Having raced both IndyCars and Formula One cars, Jacques Villeneuve is in a good position to compare the two types of racing. In his book, *Villeneuve: Winning in Style*, Jacques claims that an F1 car would be three or four seconds faster than an IndyCar doing a lap of a typical Formula One road circuit. But on a long oval like Indianapolis, according to Jacques, "the IndyCar should be faster."

"On a trickier short oval," Jacques continues, "I'm not sure which would be quicker because you could get a lot of cornering speed in the F1 car."

The IndyCar series represents a truly American form of racing and has its roots at the Indianapolis Motor Speedway in the United States. Indianapolis is the oldest race circuit still in use today. It was built in 1909 by a number of local businessmen involved in the automobile industry. The first race at Indianapolis took place on August 16, 1909, and, except for the years when America was involved in World Wars I and II, racing has taken place there every year since.

The track at Indianapolis was originally made up of crushed rock and asphalt, but this proved disastrous as the track broke up during the very first race there, causing several accidents. One driver, two riding mechanics and two spectators were killed. Before another race meet was held, the entire circuit was paved with 3.2 million bricks, giving the track its nickname, "The Brickyard."

In 1910 there were a number of race meets at Indianapolis. Each meet featured races of various lengths. The races were quite successful, but the owners wanted something more dramatic, so in 1911 they held the first Indianapolis 500.

One of the great traditions of both IndyCar and Formula One racing is the continual effort by the competitors to get around the rule book. At the time of the first Indy 500, there was a rule that every car competing had to have two people in it, a driver and a riding mechanic. The riding mechanic's job was to watch for cars coming up from behind trying to pass.

One of the drivers competing in the first Indy 500, Ray Harroun, suggested they fit his car with a mirror, so he could see behind him and thus do away with the need for a riding mechanic. This is how the first rearview mirror was born. With the weight saved by not having a riding mechanic, Harroun was able to go fast enough to win the first Indy 500.

Formula One racing has its roots in Europe, where the first Grand Prix Automobile race took place in France in 1905. Even before that, the Gordon Bennett Trophy brought teams from various countries together to compete in races that had the international flavor of today's Formula One racing.

But it was almost 50 years after the first Grand Prix

events that modern Formula One racing was actually born. In 1950, the World Drivers' Championship was introduced and races held in countries all over the world counted toward this championship.

Formula One is a truly international sport, not only because the races take place on tracks around the world, but also because the drivers and teams are associated with the countries they come from. Canadians cheer for Jacques Villeneuve, Germans cheer for Michael Schumacher, and the Italians cheer for anybody who's driving a Ferrari, no matter what country they come from!

IndyCar racing, on the other hand, takes place mainly in North America, with the bulk of the races happening in the United States, and there's no real emphasis on what country a driver is from.

There are a number of other differences between IndyCar and F1 racing, most having to do with the way the cars are built. IndyCars have developed over the years in ways that make them suitable for oval tracks. They are heavier and more powerful than F1 cars. F1 cars need to accelerate, brake, and otherwise react to driver input more quickly because they race on twisting, turning road circuits and never on ovals.

While Formula One cars have flat bottoms, IndyCars have tunnels underneath that create suction. This effectively glues the cars to the track, meaning they can corner faster without slipping.

IndyCar racing is the only automobile racing series that still allows turbocharging, which uses a car's exhaust to give it a sudden boost of power. Formula One allowed turbocharging in the 1970s and '80s, but turbocharged cars are expensive to run and by the mid-1980s only the richest F1 teams were winning races. At the end of the 1980s, to give the less wealthy teams a fair chance, turbocharging was banned from F1.

The other major differences between IndyCar and Formula One racing all come down to how the races are run and how points are awarded. Only the top six drivers crossing the finish line in a Formula One race are awarded points. In an IndyCar race, the top 12 drivers get points. Also, an additional point is given to the driver who is fastest in qualifying and the driver who leads the most laps during the race.

IndyCar races have rolling starts, meaning that the drivers follow a pace car around the track at a moderate speed and nobody is allowed to pass until the pace car pulls off, at which point the race begins. Formula One races, on the other hand, have standing starts, meaning the drivers place their cars on the starting grid and when the signal is given, the race begins.

Finally, when it rains, an IndyCar race that is being held on an oval track is postponed until the rain stops, or else canceled altogether. On road race circuits, IndyCar races go on in the rain. Formula One races always continue, no matter what the weather.

IndyCar fans will tell you that their form of racing is more exciting and competitive. In 1995, the year Jacques Villeneuve won the championship, nine different drivers won IndyCar races throughout the course of the season. Compare that to the 1997 F1season, Jacques's championship year, when only six drivers won races and twelve of the seventeen races during the season were won by either Jacques Villeneuve or Ferrari driver Michael Schumacher.

Formula One fans will argue that, while the top speed of an F1 car may be less than that of an IndyCar, and while passing opportunities are limited on many Formula One circuits, F1 is a more subtle type of racing, requiring greater inventiveness and strategy.

Whatever the differences, whichever form of racing a person enjoys, one thing is for sure: Jacques Villeneuve is a consummate racer who has thrived in both IndyCars and Formula One.

IndyCar Drivers' Points

Driver's Finish	No. of Points
1	20
2	16
3	14
4	12
5	10
6	8
7	6
8	5
9	4
10	3
11	2
12	1

Formula One Drivers' Points

Driver's Finish	No. of Points
1	10
2	6
3	4
4	3
5	2
6	1

Chapter 5

Prince of the Road

Coming out of the final turn in a practice run at the site of the Portuguese Grand Prix, Jacques Villeneuve felt something snap in the back of his car. It was about a month before Christmas and Jacques was practicing for what was to be his first season racing Formula One cars. He would drive for the Williams-Renault team, one of the best teams in the business.

When he felt his car break, he had his foot to the floor and his car was approaching 200 mph (321 km/h). The car went sideways and was on the edge of spinning out when Villeneuve flicked the steering wheel and righted it, never lifting off the accelerator at all.

"I knew it was a good lap," Villeneuve told *Maclean's* magazine afterwards, "so I didn't want to lift."

More than simply speed, Jacques Villeneuve loves being on the edge: "You could be in a plane and going very fast and that's nothing. When you feel the limits, and when, if you go over the limit, you're going to crash...it's great."

Before beginning the winter testing season with Williams-Renault, Jacques claimed he would have no difficulty getting used to the Formula One environment. After all, he'd grown up in it. He also felt confident he could learn to drive the car to its limit within the few short months he had to practice. The biggest hurdle, he figured, would be learning the tracks, most of which he had never raced on before.

He tackled the problem of learning the tracks in a typical Jacques Villeneuve manner: He went to his computer. Jacques has always loved doing things with computers, particularly playing games. In order to learn the various twists and turns on the tracks he would be racing on in 1996, he spent time playing a computer game that included realistic versions of the tracks used in Formula One.

Jacques must have practiced the computer version of the Australian Grand Prix particularly hard, because when it came to the real thing, he did a great job. The Australian Grand Prix was the first of the 1996 Formula One season and Jacques qualified faster than any of the other drivers. Only two other drivers in the history of modern Formula One racing had ever taken the first position on the starting grid in their first Formula One race.

Jacques was a little anxious about the start of the

race. He was used to competing in IndyCar races, with their rolling starts. A Formula One race begins with a standing start, and Jacques had last begun a race that way in Formula Atlantic three years earlier. But Formula Atlantic cars are smaller.

"F1 cars have three times the power," explains Jacques. "Also, in Atlantic, and before that in F3, my starts were not really a strong point because I was too excited and nervous."

Despite his concerns, he managed a perfect start in Australia and led the pack for most of the race. During a pit stop, his teammate, Damon Hill, managed to get ahead, but Jacques fought his way back and took the lead again.

Unfortunately, near the end of the race, his engine developed an oil leak and he had to slow down. Damon took advantage of Jacques's bad luck and passed him, going on to win the race. Jacques came second—not bad for his first-ever Formula One race.

Two races later, Jacques managed another second-place finish. And on April 23, two weeks after his 25th birthday, in just the fourth race of his F1 career, Jacques won his first Formula One race, the European Grand Prix at a track called Nurburgring, in Germany.

Damon Hill was first in qualifying at Nurburgring, but Jacques made a brilliant start to the race and Damon fell back into fourth place. Jacques stayed out in front for the entire race and there really wasn't much excitement until about halfway through, when a bright red car appeared in Villeneuve's rear-view mirror. It was the Ferrari of Michael Schumacher, arguably one of the greatest F1 drivers of all time, and certainly one of the most aggressive and intimidating.

Formula One racing takes place on relatively narrow, twisting, turning tracks where passing is difficult at the best of times. When one driver manages to pass another, it is often because the driver in the lead has made a mistake. As Jacques charged through the final laps at Nurburgring, Michael Schumacher was pushing hard, waiting for Villeneuve to make a mistake.

Schumacher tried on a number of occasions to get ahead of the French-Canadian, particularly when they were lapping slower traffic and Villeneuve had to slow down.

"If you get too close to a slower car at the wrong spot going into a corner," says Villeneuve, "you'll be too slow coming out of the corner. And that's when the guy coming behind you can get a run on you."

Jacques drove like a true veteran and, try as he might, Schumacher could not get by. Villeneuve won the race. Only seven drivers in the fifty-year history of Formula One racing have managed a win a race so early in their careers.

Four races later, Jacques would take to the track named after his father, the Circuit Gilles Villeneuve in Montreal, home of the Canadian Grand Prix.

Canadian racing fans came out in droves to see the native son race.

A week before the race, every last hotel room in Montreal was booked. There were a few tickets left, but already attendance was estimated at about 200,000 for three days during which practice, qualifying and the race itself would take place. This was an astounding 25 percent increase over the previous year, when Jacques wasn't in the competition.

More than 500 reporters and photographers were poised to record the homecoming of the young man with the legendary name. Jacques himself seemed to be the only one keeping a cool head.

"Of course I would like to win in Montreal," he told reporters, "but then, I would like to win every race."

Jacques drove a good race in Montreal, but he had to settle for second place behind his teammate, Damon Hill.

Jacques also took second place on what is arguably the most challenging track on the Formula One circuit. Many drivers count the Spa Francorchamps circuit in Belgium as the greatest track in modern-day racing. Jacques has described the track as very natural, following the shape of the land.

"Every lap is a big adventure," says Jacques. "It's an amazing track—majestic, beautiful, very intricate."

Spa is made up partially of roads that are used by

the public when there isn't a race going on. The track is really a throwback to the days when Grand Prix races all took place on public roads. More and more of these road circuits have been eliminated because they are considered too dangerous. They have been replaced by tracks specially built just for racing. Some of these tracks are better than others, but none quite capture the glory of the old road race circuits.

Spa is also the longest track on the F1 circuit. "By the time you get to the end of a lap," says Jacques, "you have almost forgotten what it was like when you started."

Taking second place at Spa in his first year in Formula One showed that Jacques truly has what it takes to be a successful Formula One driver.

Jacques won a total of four races during his rookie Formula One season. He crossed the finish line in second place on five occasions and took third place twice. At the end of the season, Jacques Villeneuve was second in the Formula One drivers championship, 19 points behind his teammate at Williams, Damon Hill, who won the 1996 world championship.

But it was the man who took third place in 1996, Michael Schumacher, who would prove to be Villeneuve's greatest competitor in the battle to be world champion the following year.

Jacques holds high his first major trophy, for winning the IndyCar championship in 1995.

Jacques celebrates in Victory Lane after winning the Indianapolis 500 in May 1995.

Jacques puts his Williams-Renault car through its paces during a practice session for the Brazilian Grand Prix in Sao Paulo in March 1996.

Jacques Villeneuve celebrates his victory at the Brazilian Grand Prix in traditional fashion.

Chapter 6

Getting It Together and Taking It on the Road

Frank Williams, who had a brief career as a Formula Three driver in the 1960s, became a Formula One team owner in 1969. Like many new F1 team owners, he struggled financially for his first few years. But in the late 1970s, Williams landed some solid sponsorship and his racing team has done well ever since, winning what is known as the constructors championship more times than any other team.

The constructors championship is given out at the end of each season to the team with the most combined points for its two drivers. In 1997, Williams won the constructors championship for the ninth time, which meant they had won it more times than any other team, including Ferrari, a team that has been around about a quarter century longer than Williams. It was to this highly successful team that Jacques Villeneuve came in 1996.

A great many factors go into determining who will win a Formula One race. Certainly, having the fastest car makes a difference and the car Villeneuve drove in 1996 and 1997 was definitely the fastest.

But speed isn't everything in Formula One. Another important factor is the track. Formula One race tracks wind and twist a lot and often go up and down steep hills. In 1997, there were 17 Grand Prix races on 17 completely different tracks.

On a track with long straights and high-speed corners, like Monza, home of the Italian Grand Prix, a fast car has a definite advantage. In 1971, Peter Gethin won the Italian Grand Prix averaging 150 mph (241 km/h) over the course of the race.

(Incidentally, the second-place driver that year, Ronnie Peterson, was 0.01 seconds behind Gethin, and the next three cars over the finish line were only 0.61 seconds apart, making the 1971 Italian Grand Prix the closest F1 race ever.)

The track at Monza has been changed since then, mainly to slow the cars down and make the race safer, but a fast lap around the track still averages almost 150 mph (241 km/h) and the cars get frighteningly close to 200 mph (321 km/h) in some of the straights.

On twisting, turning tracks, like the one at Monaco, the drivers are lucky if they can come close to 90 mph (145 km/h) on an average round, and the fastest cars never get a chance to use their superior speed.

In fact, racing at Monaco can be so slow at times, particularly when it is raining, that the two-hour limit on all Formula One races actually becomes a factor and the race sometimes ends before any of the drivers have had a chance to do the full number of laps. In the 62nd lap of the 1997 Monaco Grand Prix, for example, Michael Schumacher, who was more than a minute ahead of the second-place driver, slowed down considerably to make sure it would be the last lap he would have to run. The two-hour limit was reached and the race was over, even though it had been slated to go for 75 laps.

In addition to a track's layout, the condition of its surface plays a role in how well the cars perform. Some of the tracks are terribly bumpy and have less grip, so the cars jump and slip around a lot. They have to go slower to keep from going off the track.

It's tough at the best of times to pass in modern Formula One racing. All a driver can really hope for once he's in position to pass is that the driver ahead of him will make a mistake on a corner. Only then can one car nip inside the other and pass. Passing on the outside of a turn is almost unheard of. But in the second to last race of the 1996 season, Michael Schumacher got a bit of a shock when he was passed by Jacques Villeneuve on the outside of a 120-mph (193-km/h) curve.

"I was looking for him in my mirrors," Schumacher said afterward, "but I couldn't find him. Suddenly he appeared alongside me."

Jacques, being his usual self, says he just did it for a bit of a lark. "It was fun overtaking on the outside," he claimed. "I told the team that I thought I could do it, so they responded by saying they would come and pick me out of the guardrail if I tried."

In order to win at the Formula One game, a driver has to take risks, be aggressive, and outsmart the other drivers, which is exactly what Villeneuve did when he took Schumacher on the outside.

Weather also plays an important role in determining the outcome of a Formula One race. Unlike IndyCar races, Formula One Grands Prix are run come rain or shine. Some F1 drivers, like Michael Schumacher and the late Ayrton Senna, are famous for their awesome ability to drive in the rain.

Villeneuve, on the other hand, is not considered an exceptional wet-weather driver. He didn't do all that well in any of the 1997 races that saw rain. Halfway through the season, in a wet French Grand Prix, Villeneuve was only able to power his mighty Williams machine over the line in fourth place. Four races later, the Belgian Grand Prix also saw rain, and Villeneuve managed only fifth.

Earlier in the season, at the Monaco Grand Prix, rain was again a factor, but this time strategy also played an important role. Believing that the rain would stop and the track would dry out, Villeneuve and the other Williams driver, Frentzen, went out on dry-weather tires. The rain didn't stop, however, and Villeneuve and Frentzen slipped and slid all over the still-wet track. By lap 15 Villeneuve found himself in the humiliating position of being lapped by Michael Schumacher.

Luck is another important factor in Grand Prix racing, and Villeneuve was incredibly lucky in a number of 1997 Grand Prix races. In the second race, the Brazilian Grand Prix, Jacques managed to capture the first-place position on the starting grid, but Michael Schumacher's Ferrari was second, right next to him. As the two cars came into the first corner, Schumacher managed to put his car on the inside. There was less grip on the outside of the track where Jacques was running and, in a desperate attempt to get ahead of Schumacher, Jacques skidded off the track.

He managed to get his car back onto the circuit, but some of the gravel at the side of the track had flown up into the cockpit and Jacques was sitting on a piece of it. He was quite relieved when the race had to be stopped because one of the drivers had stalled and was sitting in a dangerous spot on the track.

On the second start, knowing he had the faster car, Villeneuve played it cool and let Schumacher have the first corner. At the beginning of lap two, Villeneuve overtook Schumacher and he never looked back. He took the checkered flag after leading the race for all but a couple of laps.

Jacques likes to describe his racing career as simply another job. But Formula One is a job where you don't often hear of an employee calling in sick. Three races into the 1997 season, at the Argentinean Grand Prix, Jacques had a bad case of stomach flu that severely reduced his stamina. He was afraid he might not be able to handle the two grueling hours it takes to complete a Formula One Grand Prix. But Jacques prevailed, driving fastest in qualifying and then going on to win the race. Villeneuve had proven that he was able to "drive through a problem" and do his job.

During the British Grand Prix, Villeneuve encountered some bad luck of a mechanical nature. When he made his first pit stop, one of his front wheels stuck. He was in the pit lane for about 30 seconds, 20 seconds longer than he should have been, and when he came back out onto the track he was in seventh place.

Jacques said afterward he was certain he would never be able to catch race leader Michael Schumacher. The race in Britain was an important one. Michael Schumacher had won the last two races and was 14 points ahead of Villeneuve in world championship points. But the German pulled out of the race about halfway through when his car broke down.

Jacques managed to claw his way back into second place, but it didn't look as though he would be able to catch first-place Mika Hakinnen. Jacques's good luck was in full force, however, and with only seven laps to go, Hakinnen's engine blew. Villeneuve crossed the finish line first.

Two races later, in Hungary, with only two laps to go, Jacques was in second place again, but was an impossible 30 seconds behind race leader Damon Hill. The track in Hungary is a tight, winding one that is notoriously difficult to pass on. Only once in the track's 12-year history has the Hungarian Grand Prix been won by someone who didn't start the race in one of the top three positions.

Even if Villeneuve could catch Hill, his chances of getting by were practically nil. Suddenly, Damon slowed down and started swerving from side to side. He had had a mechanical failure and found he could only keep the car going by steering back and forth. Jacques sailed by and won the race, with Hill lucky to limp home second.

Even the fastest car will perform badly if it isn't set up properly. There are many engine and body parts on a Formula One car that can be adjusted, and the possible combinations are practically endless. How a driver and his mechanics set up the car is determined by the characteristics of the track they are racing on and by the weather on race day.

The amount of downforce—the amount of downward air pressure on the vehicle—can be adjusted by changing the size and angle of the wings on the front and back of the car. High downforce will make the car slower overall, but it will make it faster in the corners because it will slide less easily. The trick is to get the balance exactly right for each different track.

Balance is the key when it comes to adjusting the other parts on the car as well. During practice in the days immediately before a Grand Prix event, a driver will do a few laps and then come into the pit to work with his crew of mechanics adjusting his car's setup.

Just about everything on a Formula One car is adjustable. In the engine, the amount of air that is mixed with the fuel can be altered. The gears in the transmission can be changed. Having the tires at exactly the right pressure is essential to get them to perform at their best. The suspension can be made harder or softer. Cooling ducts can be opened more or less, depending on the weather, to keep the engine and brakes performing at their optimum temperature. The entire car can be raised or lowered to change the amount of space between its bottom and the ground.

Previous experience at a particular race track can play an important role in getting the setup right for a particular circuit, but in the end it comes down to the driver and how well he can explain what he needs to his crew. Indeed, Formula One fans will argue that, while the weather, the track, and the speed and setup of the car are important, the single most important factor in Grand Prix racing is the driver.

Jacques Villeneuve is a good driver. Not only is he fast and consistent, but he works well with a team. He is able to explain to his mechanics what he needs from his car and thus help them get the setup just right. He takes advantage of his luck. He drives through problems, rather than let them distract or upset him. Perhaps most important of all to his fans, Jacques is a nice guy. He's aggressive when necessary and has learned to take care of himself on the race track, but he also shows the other drivers respect, both on and off the track.

With a fast car and a great driver like Jacques, the Williams team looked set to capture the 1997 Formula One world championship.

Chapter 7

King of the Road—Junior

Jacques Villeneuve was the fourth-fastest driver on the track at the end of the first day of practice for the Australian Grand Prix, the first race of the 1997 season. This was not such a fantastic result for the driver who went faster than any of the others in qualifying in Australia the year before.

But Jacques wasn't particularly worried. He knew his Renault engine was capable of propelling his car to a much better result.

What did bother him, according to Craig Pollock, Villeneuve's manager, "was watching Frentzen [his teammate, who was second fastest] strutting around with his chest puffed out." Jacques told Pollock he was determined to "destroy" Frentzen in qualifying.

Formula One commentator Gerald Donaldson claims Villeneuve was merely toying with his rivals on that first day in Australia.

"The most successful competitors in the F1 game," claims Donaldson, "employ psychological trickery to outwit and or unsettle opponents."

On that first day of practice in Australia, every time he approached the finish line where the timing device would clock his speed, Villeneuve either deliberately slowed down or pulled off the track into the pit lane.

Then, for official qualifying on Saturday, Villeneuve suddenly pulled out all the stops. He drove the car to its absolute limit, taking corners as fast as he could without spinning, rapidly shifting the car up through its gears in the straights to approach speeds of 175 mph (281 km/h).

When it was all over and the starting order had been decided, Villeneuve was more than two seconds faster than any of the drivers on the other teams. This is a sport where the top half-dozen drivers in qualifying are often only tenths or even hundredths of a second apart. It was a devastating blow for the other drivers to find out that Villeneuve's car was so fast.

But having the fastest car in qualifying is a far cry from winning a Grand Prix race, and Jacques encountered some bad luck in the first race of the 1997 season. Sandwiched between two other cars at the first corner, where there was really only enough room for one, Jacques was pushed off the track and out of the race.

Jacques blamed Ferrari driver Eddie Irvine for putting him off the track in Australia. He claimed that Irvine tried to pass in a situation where passing was impossible. What really bothered Jacques, however, was not so much Irvine's driving, but his failure to accept blame. Irvine maintained afterward that he had made a legitimate attempt to pass and that the result was an unavoidable racing incident. The racing authorities apparently agreed, because no action was taken against any of the drivers.

A driver named David Coulthard won the Australian Grand Prix, but it was the second-place driver, the German named Michael Schumacher, driving the bright red Ferrari, who would ultimately give Jacques the greatest run for his money as the season progressed.

Jacques put his Williams powerhouse to good use in the next two races, winning both the Brazilian and the Argentinean Grands Prix. But he had mechanical problems in the following two races in San Marino and Monaco and was unable to finish either of them.

Meanwhile, Schumacher came second in San Marino and he won the Grand Prix of Monaco. This put him ahead in world championship points, with 24 to Villeneuve's 20.

Jacques proceeded to pull back into the lead in points by winning the Spanish Grand Prix. Schumacher was only able to scare up three points with his fourth-place finish.

The next race was Jacques's home race in Canada, at the track in Montreal named for his father. Jacques was determined to win at the Circuit Gilles Villeneuve.

Although he was unable to beat Schumacher in qualifying, Jacques managed to put his Williams on the front row of the starting grid by qualifying second. Unfortunately, he pushed too hard at the start of the race and spun into a wall as he came around to finish the first lap.

Perhaps the pressure had been too much. Before the Canadian Grand Prix, Villeneuve had been greeted in his home country by huge throngs of fans and a great deal of media attention. He must have felt a terrible sense of disappointment when he failed to complete even one lap of the race.

Perhaps to cheer himself up, or maybe to draw attention away from his disappointing result in the Canadian Grand Prix, Jacques went out in the days after the race and had his hair bleached blond. He said he did it so that he would not be recognized everywhere he went, but it had quite the opposite effect. Photos of the new-look Villeneuve were splashed all over newspapers and magazines.

Schumacher won the race in Canada and then went on to win again in France. This put the German 14 points ahead of Villeneuve in the battle to be world champion. This was, however, the largest lead Schumacher would be able to manage.

The next race in Britain was held on Sunday, July

13, exactly 20 years to the day after Gilles Villeneuve raced in his first Grand Prix. Jacques celebrated the occasion by picking up 10 points for the win and giving the Williams team their 100th Grand Prix victory. Michael Schumacher scored no points as his Ferrari suffered a mechanical failure and he couldn't finish the race.

It was Villeneuve's turn to retire at the German Grand Prix as he spun out of the race. Schumacher was second, putting him ten points ahead of Villeneuve.

In Hungary Jacques won, and Michael was fourth. This closed the gap between the two drivers to only three points.

The Belgium Grand Prix saw rain. Schumacher, as usual, drove a brilliant race. At one point he was more than a minute ahead of the second-place driver. He crossed the finish line almost half a minute ahead of his closest competitor. Jacques managed fifth and was now eleven points back of Schumacher.

Jacques was fifth again in Italy, but this time he was ahead of Michael Schumacher, who could manage only sixth.

It was at this point, three-quarters of the way through the season, that Jacques Villeneuve turned things around. He won back-to-back races in Austria and Luxembourg, while Schumacher managed only sixth in Austria and a crash in Luxembourg. Jacques was now the leader in world championship points, with 77 to Schumacher's 68.

Coming into the second-last race of the season, in Japan, Jacques ran into some trouble during a practice session when he passed another car while a yellow flag was out. A yellow flag means all drivers on the track must slow down and no car may pass another. Jacques had passed under a yellow flag at another practice session earlier in the season and had received a warning at the time. Now, because this was his second offense, officials decided to ban Jacques from the Japanese Grand Prix.

Villeneuve was allowed to race in Japan pending an appeal of the ban. He managed to cross the finish line in fifth position, but he was later disqualified from the results when his appeal didn't go through.

Meanwhile, Michael Schumacher won the race, putting him back in the lead for the world championship, but only by a single point. The 1997 Formula One world championship would be decided at the final race of the season, the European Grand Prix in Jerez, Spain.

Michael Schumacher is considered by many to be the greatest Formula One driver of all time. He is also considered by many to be the bad boy of Formula One racing. He has, almost single-handedly, turned Formula One racing into what could be described as a contact sport. He bumps other cars, blocks ruthlessly when someone tries to pass, and pushes his way aggressively around the track.

Schumacher won the 1994 world championship by a knockout when he pushed English driver Damon Hill off the track as Damon tried to pass. As the drivers lined up for the European Grand Prix on October 26, 1997, many Villeneuve fans were afraid Schumacher might get up to his old tricks again.

The battle to be world champion was shaping up to be a good one as qualifying saw an unheard of three-way tie. Villeneuve, Schumacher and Frentzen all did a lap of the track in exactly 1 minute, 21.072 seconds. Villeneuve was the first to manage this time, and by Formula One rules, this put him in first position at the start of the race. Schumacher was right beside him in second place. Racing fans couldn't have asked for a better start to what promised to be a fantastic event.

Schumacher got away well, coming into the first corner ahead of Villeneuve. Jacques kept pace, but was unable to get close enough to pass. There were about five seconds separating the two drivers when they both came in for their first pit stops. Coming out of the pits, Villeneuve was less than a second behind Schumacher and Schumacher couldn't shake the French Canadian. After the second round of pit stops, Villeneuve was still right behind the German.

Then, on lap 47, at a sharp right-hand corner called

Dry Sack, Michael Schumacher went wide. Villeneuve saw his chance. He cut inside and got ready to pull ahead. Suddenly, Schumacher veered right, slamming into the side of Villeneuve's car and tossing it up into the air.

"I was not really surprised when he finally decided to turn in on me," said Villeneuve after the race. "It was a little bit expected, and I knew I was taking a bit of a risk. But when he touched me, it was a really big impact, and I was worried that something might have broken. For the rest of the race, my car felt strange."

Ramming his car into Villeneuve's turned out to be a disastrous move for Schumacher. He went careening off the track and into the gravel where his wheels stuck. He was out of the race and had to sit at the side of the track and watch while the other drivers flew by.

Despite being hit by Schumacher, Jacques managed to keep his car on the track. All he had to do to take the world championship now was to finish in the points. Jacques not only made it to the end of the race, he held onto the lead until the final lap when two drivers came through to pass. Jacques picked up four points as he crossed the finish line in third place.

Jacques Villeneuve was the new Formula One world champion. He had shown the world he was capable of beating everyone, even someone as talented and ruthless as Michael Schumacher.

Villeneuve had become the first Canadian ever to

win the Formula One world championship. Not only that, he was the first driver of any nationality to win all three of the top international motor racing championships—the Formula One, the CART IndyCar, and the Indianapolis 500.

Villeneuve had arrived. Having the best car on the track in 1997 had certainly made a difference, but few people would question his ability as a race car driver. He had made his mark, in more ways than one. As he arrived back at the Williams garage after his victory, he found members of his team and his friends all wearing yellow wigs in a celebration of Jacques's own peroxide-blond hair.

Chapter 8

The King Gives Up His Crown

Toward the end of the 1998 season, it was quite clear that Jacques Villeneuve was going to have to give up his world championship crown to either Mika Hakinnen or Michael Schumacher. The French Canadian was asked if he had a preference about which driver should succeed him. Villeneuve grinned. "I sure do," he told sports writer Gerald Donaldson. "But I only discuss that with my friends."

He went on to give Hakinnen a little advice. He said that Mika should "stay focused and watch himself." Jacques explained that while he didn't know Mika very well, he did know that the Finn played fair. "Everybody should be like that."

Jacques obviously hadn't forgotten Michael Schumacher's failed attempt to take him out of the final race of the 1997 season.

After a great deal of controversy and a formal inquiry, Formula One authorities stripped Schumacher of all his 1997 points as punishment for what they decided was a deliberate attempt to take Villeneuve out of the last race of the 1997 season.

But Villeneuve didn't think having his points taken away would change the German driver. "You don't change someone's personality," Villeneuve said. "I was brought up believing you should behave in the right way so you can sleep at night. Michael doesn't seem to care about such things."

Still, Michael Schumacher is a supremely talented driver. Over the course of 1997, he managed to challenge a car that started off the year two seconds faster than his Ferrari. The question remained: was Villeneuve's early success in Formula One due mainly to the fact that he was driving for the team with the fastest cars?

It makes a difference, of course. If the car is not competitive, the driver doesn't stand a chance, no matter how good he is. If Williams fielded exceptional cars in 1996 and 1997, their 1998 car was a dud. Villeneuve struggled all year to remain competitive. Many would say he did a great job considering what he had to work with.

In the first race of the season, Jacques qualified fourth and finished fifth. Not a great finish, but it was to be his best for a while. At the second race in Brazil, he came away with no points as he managed only seventh place. On lap 52 of the Argentinean Grand Prix, as Villeneuve struggled to hold onto sixth place,

David Coulthard tried to pass him. The two cars connected and Villeneuve spun out of the race.

At San Marino, Villeneuve finally managed to pick up a few more points as he had his best finish yet. He made a great start to the race, immediately overtaking two cars and putting himself in fourth place. Unfortunately, he could manage no better, and fourth place is where he finished the race. At the Spanish Grand Prix, he picked up another point as he crossed the finish line in sixth place. He was fifth at Monaco.

Back at home, at the Circuit Gilles Villeneuve in Montreal, he could only manage tenth. He did much better in France, finishing fourth. The British Grand Prix was a bit of a disappointment. Villeneuve did a wonderful job of qualifying, putting himself in the third position on the grid, but he finished the race just outside the points in seventh place.

Jacques picked up a single point with a sixth-place finish in Austria. In Germany, after ten races, Jacques finally managed to make it to the podium with a third-place finish. He indicated after the race that he hoped finishing on the podium was going to become a trend. Indeed, in the following race, he was on the same step of the podium, taking third place in the Hungarian Grand Prix.

The Hungarian race was particularly rewarding for Jacques. He had been able to reach the podium despite having his power steering fail 10 laps into the race. Like most Formula One drivers, Jacques undergoes fairly heavy physical training to stay in shape. His fitness paid off as he steered the car manually for 67 laps.

The weekend in Belgium was something of a disaster for Jacques. During a practice session the day before the race at the famed Belgian race track, Spa Francorchamps, Jacques lost control at a corner named Eau Rouge, one of the most challenging corners on the Grand Prix circuit. Traveling at about 170 mph (273 km/h), he crashed backwards into a tire barrier.

Jacques, who bruised his knee in the incident, made light of it. "This was easily my best crash in Formula One," he said. "I thought, 'This is going to hurt,' and it did."

In the race itself, only eight cars made it to the finish line. Jacques was not one of them. Although it was not raining at the start of the race, the track was wet from an earlier downpour. Before the first lap was over, 14 cars had plowed into one another in a pile-up that occurred when David Coulthard lost control. The race was stopped and it took nearly an hour to clear up the wreckage.

By lap 7 of the restarted race, the rain had started again. Villeneuve was in fifth place when he lost control on lap 17. He crashed into the barriers and out of the race.

In Italy, Villeneuve lost control again, this time on

a dry track, and spun out just over halfway through the race as he tried to catch Ferrari driver Eddie Irvine.

Jacques managed to finish the Luxembourg Grand Prix, but eighth was the best he could do. After Luxembourg, there was an unusual five-week gap until the final race in Japan and Jacques used it to unwind. He was in his race car only once during that time.

"It's good because I'm fresher now," Villeneuve said before the Japanese Grand Prix. "I want to have fun and drive."

Villeneuve's idea of unwinding, however, didn't involve sitting around at home in Monaco. During the five weeks between races he traveled to Berlin, Moscow, Paris, Montreal, New York, and Hollywood.

Jacques crossed the finish line in sixth place in Japan and thus secured a fifth-place finish in world championship points.

"This race was like the last day of school," Villeneuve said after the race. With the season finished, and Finnish driver Mika Hakinnen taking the world championship, Jacques was ready to party.

Jacques said the 1998 season had brought some frustration, but also hard work. Despite having an uncompetitive car, the team had carried on and improved throughout the season.

Jacques has always been proud of how hard he works. He has also emphasized the importance of the team effort, and 1998 was no exception in this respect. He will tell you without hesitating that he always drives to win, but if winning isn't possible, he takes satisfaction out of knowing he and his team have done the best they possibly could.

Four-time world champion Alain Prost, who now owns a Formula One team, said that he thought Villeneuve had showed great character fighting so hard in what was ultimately a losing battle.

"It's nice when you have been perceived the way you really are," says Villeneuve about the comment by Prost. "I worked a lot harder than I did last year, both in the car and in training."

As the 1998 season progressed, it became apparent that Williams would be losing their world championship driver the following year. A new Formula One team was in the works. It would be called British American Racing (BAR for short), and one of the key players in getting the team off the ground was Craig Pollock, Jacques's manager.

Jacques claimed that his manager's involvement in the team did not automatically mean he would drive for BAR. He said that he wanted to join a competitive team with people who worked well together. In the end, Jacques decided that BAR was going to be just such a team, and he signed up to drive for them.

Despite a disappointing 1998 season, Jacques maintained his optimism for the future. In one of the

Web sites dedicated to him, Jacques was quoted as saying that he cannot be happy with his fifth-place result in 1998.

"My goal remains to win races," he said. "I'm optimistic for the future and impatient to start this new challenge."

Chapter 9

Driving Forward

Jacques Villeneuve hasn't let the glamour and fame of being a Formula One driver go to his head. Not too much, anyway.

It's true, he has been seen in the company of actor Sylvester Stallone, who is a great race fan and who is said to be working on a movie about Formula One racing. He's also been seen with a number of pretty glamourous ladies.

During the first race weekend of 1999, at the Australian Grand Prix, Jacques was caught off guard when two women he had been dating over the preceding few months showed up in the race paddock at the same time. According to *Toronto Star* race reporter Gerald Donaldson, exotic British musician Vanessa-Mae and Australian actress and pop singer Natalie Imbruglia both arrived to say hello to Jacques and to cheer him on.

Jacques had recently broken up with his steady girlfriend of many years, Sandrine Gros d'Aillon.

Since then he had been linked with a series of female celebrities, including tennis star Martina Hingis. He says he would like to have a family one day, but is too busy for a serious relationship at present.

"I have no time to court a woman. At any rate, not like I imagine it ought to be done, with flowers and surprise visits," he told *enRoute* magazine. "I'm gone too often."

Jacques continues to claim that he is just a normal guy trying to have some fun. If this is the case, then British American Racing (BAR) might be just the team for Jacques. BAR boss and Villeneuve manager Craig Pollock has been quoted as saying that the important thing during the team's first year is for everybody to have some fun.

If having fun costs money, BAR should be able to buy quite a bit. BAR's main sponsor, British American Tobacco, has reportedly pledged $80 million a year for the next five years to make sure the team has everything it needs. The cars will be built by Reynard, the company that supplied the IndyCar equipment Villeneuve used so successfully in 1994 and 1995. They will be engineered and built in a brand new, 80,000–square foot factory in Brackley, England.

A fair portion of BAR's budget will go to Jacques himself. Initial reports have pegged his salary at $15 million, plus bonuses if he gets results.

"The budget is there," says Villeneuve of the new

team. "The technology is there, the manpower, the knowledge. So there is no reason for it not to work. We should be competitive."

But Villeneuve insists that money isn't everything. He says he cares most about racing for a competitive team and that the most important factor in being competitive is teamwork.

"The reason I've signed with BAR is because I believe in the people . . . It is important to know with whom you are going to work [and] that the chemistry will be right."

When BAR first announced that it would race in Formula One in 1999, there was talk of winning races their first season out, maybe even the first race in Australia. At the official unveiling of BAR's new car, Villeneuve told reporters that there were those who wanted to see the upstart team fail. He didn't mind though, because "having people against you makes it more fun when you win."

But as the 1999 season drew closer, the talk became less optimistic. During winter testing in Spain, pieces of the new BAR car flew off. Jacques lost the rear wing and the engine cover while testing the car at high speeds. After the car fell apart, Jacques supposedly roared into the pits, and calmly told the team, "She's fast."

On the weekend of the Australian Grand Prix, Jacques admitted that the team had not had time to practice their pit stops. Formula One races are often won and lost in the pits, so the chances of BAR doing well in Australia were becoming more and more unlikely.

Jacques was eleventh fastest in qualifying for the Australian Grand Prix—pretty fast for a brand new team, but certainly not fast enough to catch the likes of McLaren, the team that won both the constructors and the drivers championships in 1998.

In the race itself, Jacques managed to get himself up into seventh place before his car fell apart on him. He was doing about 170 mph (273 km/h) on a gradual curve when the back wing flew off. Without the downforce provided by the wing, the back end of his car slipped out from under him and he spun. He glanced off a wall before finally coming to a stop. He didn't hurt himself, but his race was finished.

No doubt Jacques will work hard as he has in the past and he and the team will improve to the point where BAR is a contender for the world championship. It might not happen in 1999, but certainly early in the new millennium.

Meanwhile, Villeneuve remains hugely popular all over the world: in Italy because of his name, in France because of the language he speaks, and in Canada—where he won the 1997 Lou Marsh Trophy as Canada's top athlete—because he's Canadian. Elsewhere he is popular just because he is Jacques

Villeneuve and no other Formula One driver is quite the same.

To some, his immense popularity might seem at odds with his obvious desire to maintain a certain distance from the media and from his fans. He seems, in many ways, to be something of a solitary figure. His sports of choice, skiing and motor racing, both involve speed, certainly, but they are also both sports in which one man stands alone in competition against others.

In his review of the 1996 Formula One season in *Road and Track* magazine, Rob Walker pegged Villeneuve as a loner "who enjoys his seclusion." Walker goes on to explain that he ran into Villeneuve in a washroom in Portugal and "he was wearing his helmet," most likely to keep reporters like Walker from asking him questions.

When Villeneuve isn't racing, he enjoys other solitary activities such as playing on his computer or reading a good book.

"I can just read a good book and I am happy," he told the Reuters News Agency. "In a plane, I hate someone bugging me when I'm reading."

Jacques particularly enjoys science fiction novels, including *The Tale of the Eternal Champion* series by British author Michael Moorcock.

Music is another favorite pastime. Jacques likes listening to selections from his large and eclectic collection of CDs. He also plays the guitar and has even written some songs. He plans to build his own recording studio one day and record his compositions.

In 1995, Jacques's girlfriend at the time, Sandrine Gros d'Aillon, told reporter James Deacon that Jacques needs his downtime or he becomes too hyper. "He is more afraid of the glamour than he is of [crashing his car into] the wall," she said.

These days, Jacques may be a little less intimidated by the glamour of Formula One, but he still seems to want to keep himself out of the public eye to some extent.

Jacques claims that he doesn't want to shut out his public, he simply wants to make sure that he honors his first priority: racing cars.

"If you overdo it," he once told a reporter, "the racing suffers and then you will be nothing."

Glossary of
Motor Racing Terms

constructors championship—championship won by the Formula One team with the most combined points. Each Formula One team fields two drivers. At the end of each season the points these two drivers have scored are added together to determine the winner of the constructors championship.

F1—a short form of Formula One.

flag—Flags are waved at drivers by race officials to give the drivers information and instructions during races. The black flag tells a specific driver to pull off the track into his pit and stop racing for a period of time. The black flag is used when a driver has been given a *stop-and-go penalty* (see below).

The checkered flag is waved at each of the drivers as they cross the finish line. To say a driver "took the checkered flag" means the driver won the race.

grid—the order in which the drivers start a race; also refers to the markings on the track indicating where each driver is to position his car before the start of a race. Because there are more than 20 cars in most Formula One races and because the tracks are much too narrow to have the drivers start side by side (the way runners do in foot races) cars start the race lined up in staggered rows of two based on their qualifying times. Two cars line up side by side at the front of the grid, the next two cars line up behind them, and so on to the back of the line.

lifting—taking the foot off the gas pedal, thus slowing the car. Because Formula One cars race at such high speeds and are often quite close together during a race, lifting at a place on the track where other drivers might not expect a car to slow down can be almost as dangerous as putting on the brakes.

outbrake—waiting longer to put on the brakes coming into a curve. With Formula One cars very evenly matched, and Formula One race tracks winding and curving so much, it is close to impossible for one car to pass another on the relatively short sections of straight track. Passing usually takes place at turns in the track where the drivers must put on the brakes to slow down. When one driver gets by another by waiting to put on the brakes coming into a curve, that driver is said to have "outbraked" his opponent.

pace car—a road car that comes out onto the track when there is some danger, usually after an accident has left debris on the track. All the racers must slow down and stay behind the pace car, and no driver may pass another while the pace car is on the track. The pace car doesn't come out very often in Formula One, especially in comparison to IndyCar racing.

Having the pace car on the track can be a great advantage to drivers who are not doing too well in a race, because it forces the cars to bunch up close together. If the lead driver in a race has managed to open up a big gap between himself and the second-place car, for example, the second-place car can close that gap and get right in behind the first-place car while the pace car is out. When the pace car leaves the track and racing resumes, the second-place car will be in a better position to pass the driver in front.

paddock—the area near each race track where the drivers stay during a race weekend. Each driver has a trailer where he can stay when he isn't out on the track practicing, qualifying or racing in his car. In modern Formula One racing the paddock is often fenced off to keep fans and unwanted media people out.

parade lap (formation lap)—lap around the track that takes place after the race cars line up on the track, but before they begin the actual race. The drivers go around in the order they *qualified* (see below). No driver is allowed to pass another during the parade lap. After the parade lap, they line up on the *grid* (see above) to begin the race.

pit lane—a short section of track running next to the actual race track parallel to the finish line. Each team has an area—a pit—in the pit lane where they keep equipment and workers to change the tires on their cars, add fuel and do minor repairs during the course of a race. When a driver needs fuel or new tires, he pulls into the pit lane and parks his car in the area designated for his team.

There is a speed limit in the pit lane. As a driver pulls into the pits he pushes a button on the steering wheel that limits how fast the car can go and keeps it within the pit lane speed limit.

podium—the platform where the first-, second- and third-place drivers stand to receive their trophies after a race. To say a driver had a "podium finish" simply means he finished first, second or third in the race.

pole position—the best place to be on the track at the start of a race. The driver who goes around the track fastest during *qualifying* (see below) starts the race in the pole position, which is at the front of the starting lineup, on the inside. Being on the inside is good because it means the driver has a slightly shorter distance to travel going around the first curve in the track.

qualifying—event the day before the race to decide the order the drivers start the race in. During qualifying, each car comes out onto the track to do some laps, and these laps are timed.

During qualifying the drivers try to go around the track as fast as possible. The one who drives around the track in the shortest time—the one who went once around the track the fastest, in other words—gets to be in the *pole position* (see above) for the race. The second fastest driver starts next to him. The third and fourth fastest drivers start side by side behind the two fastest, and so on by twos to the back of the line.

stop-and-go penalty—a form of punishment given a driver who has broken a rule during a race. The driver must pull off the track and keep his car in the *pit lane* (see above) for a certain number of seconds.

If the penalty calls for 10 seconds in the pit lane, the driver will lose between 20 and 30 seconds in the race because of the time it takes him to slow to a stop and then accelerate back up to speed after he has served his penalty.

Research Sources

Canadian Press. "Villeneuve optimistic about BAR's chances," *Toronto Star*, January 5 1999, page E9.

Deacon, James. "In the driver's seat: Jacques Villeneuve is racing's hottest commodity," *Maclean's*, August 14, 1995, page 44.

———. "Jacques Villeneuve: Speeding to the top," *Maclean's*, December 18, 1995, page 64.

Donaldson, Gerald. *Gilles Villeneuve: The Life of the Legendary Racing Driver*. Toronto: McClelland & Stewart, 1989.

———. "V is for Victory: Villeneuve's Formula Could Rule the World," *Toronto Star*, March 2, 1997, page C1.

———. "Villeneuve likes to play head games with his rivals," *Toronto Star*, March 21, 1997, page D12.

———. "Villeneuve unveils his new wheels," *Toronto Star*, January 7 1999, page D24.

Gale Infobase, August 1997. "Jacques Villeneuve" facts.

Germain, George-Hébert. "Jacques Be Quick/Contre la Montre," *enRoute*, June 1999, p. 33.

Henry, Alan. "Coming soon: Adrian Reynard as BAT-man," *Road & Track*, March 1998, page 136.

———. "Jacques steals home as Micheal strikes out", *Road & Track*, January 1998, page 150.

Huff, Richard. *Formula One Racing*. Philadelphia: Chelsea House Publishers, 1998.

Jones, Bruce. *The Official ITV Formula One 1997 Grand Prix Guide*. Vancouver: Raincoast Books, 1997.

Richler, Jacob. "Jacques Attack," *Saturday Night*, September 1995, page 30.

Toronto Star, (with files from Ken McKee). "Canuck on pole for F1," March 8, 1997, page B6.

Villeneuve, Jacques with Gerald Donaldson. *Villeneuve: Winning in Style.*. London: CollinsWillow (imprint of HarperCollins Publishers), 1996/1997 .

Wade, Stephen. "New racing team lowers the bar," Associated Press (*Globe and Mail*, January 7, 1999, page S5).

Walker, Rob. "An Excellent First Half," *Road and Track*, November 1997.

Warwick, Liz. "Native son returns: Jacques Villeneuve revs up Montreal race fans," *Maclean's*, June 17, 1996, page 43.

Watkins, Sid. *Triumph and Tragedy in Formula One: Story of Professor Sid Watkins*. London: Motorbooks International, 1996.

Look for these other

CHAMPION SPORT

B I O G R A P H I E S

Tennis

- Martina Hingis
- Pete Sampras

Soccer

- Maradona
- Ronaldo

Formula One Racing

- Michael Schumacher

Basketball

- Michael Jordan
- Shaquille O'Neal

Boxing

- Muhammad Ali

Figure Skating

- Tara Lipinski

We hoped you enjoyed reading this book. We welcome your comments. Please contact us:

Warwick Publishing
162 John Street, 3rd Floor
Toronto, Ontario, Canada
M5V 2E5

Telephone: (416) 596-1555

FAX: (416) 596-1520

Website: www.warwickgp.com

E-Mail: mbrooke@warwickgp.com